UNRAVELING

Poems by

Mildred Santiago-Vélez

BookLocker

Saint Petersburg, Florida

ISBN: 978-1-64438-086-4

Published by BookLocker.com, Inc., St. Petersburg, Florida.

Printed on acid-free paper.

BookLocker.com, Inc.
2019

First Edition

Library of Congress Cataloging in Publication Data
Santiago-Vélez, Mildred
Unraveling by Mildred Santiago-Vélez
POETRY/American/Hispanic American | FICTION/Women | SELF
HELP/Personal Growth/Self-Esteem
Library of Congress Control Number: 2019913334

"A poem begins with a lump in the throat, a sense of wrong, a homesickness or a love sickness. It is a reaching-out toward expression; an effort to find fulfillment. A complete poem is one where an emotion has found its thought and the thought has found words."

Robert Frost

ACKNOWLEDGEMENT

Heartfelt thanks to my friend and former colleague, Mary López-Adams and the Legacy of Leesburg Writing Circle; their input and enthusiasm motivated me to publish my poems.

CONTENTS

1. IDENTITY UNFOLDING

"You get older
and you are a whole mess of things,
new thoughts, sorry feeling,
big plans, enormous doubts,
going along hoping and getting disappointed,
over and over again,
no wonder I don't recognize
my little crayon picture.
It appears to be me,
and it is not."

Virginia Euwer Wolff, <u>*True Believer*</u>

Identity

To know who we are,
is to know our history.
To understand why we speak the way we do,
is to know our past.
To decipher why we dance the way we do,
and why we love the way we do, or
why we eat the foods we do,
is to know our roots.

I dug here and there trying to find my roots
and uncovered them
in the Caribbean island of Boriquén,
at one time the land of the brave,
home to the Taino people.
Peaceful, hospitable, generous, soft-spoken people
who lived in harmony, united by language
and spiritual beliefs, all within a social order.
A distinct culture, I would say,
certainly not savages.

Peace & tranquility abruptly ended
when the Spaniards arrived in search of riches.
The placid, brave people fought & resisted
but soon were ravaged by those who claimed
superior stance and culture.
The Taino men were decimated, the women
forcefully taken by white Spaniards.
Over time a new order, a new society came to be.

The hunt for gold and riches ended,
another wave of Spaniards settled the island.
This time they came to farm and work hard;
they married their own and the mestizos too.
Their Spanish language dominated,
but not all was lost, rather,
the ways & doings of two cultures
were wondrously, though painful at times,

interwoven, slowly
moving toward a new world culture.

The evolution did not end.
The need for laborers was great,
sugar plantations were growing, and
so it was that free men from African tribes,
Yoruba, Igbo, and Bantu,
were brought to the island against their will;
free men forced into slavery.
Once again, over time, &
in keeping with the ebbs & flows of life,
the Africans too began to marry
Taino & mestiza women;
another strong culture was
now mingling & mixing with
the already complex people of Boriquén.
It was inevitable, history in the making,
the evidence is palpable.
African cultural practices,
words & beliefs are integral components
of our now compounded island nation
known as Puerto Rico.

Who am I?
A product of my interwoven past
with a language enriched by many &
a culture, diverse & abounding, that
makes up the colorful,
at times complex
mosaic of my identity.
I am not Taina,
I am not Spaniard,
I am not African.
I am a fusion of these,
unique & whole.
Their roots are in my blood,
their history imbues my existence.

I am Puerto Rico and
its complex, unique composition.
I am New York,
another amalgam of cultures.
Who am I?
Be it known that most of all,
I am a Latina of the Americas.

Immortal Woman

Ever since prehistoric times
Woman has been dragged, pushed, pulled,
belittled, enslaved, raped, disregarded, & discarded;
her wild seed trampled.
Neither time nor history has changed
Woman's destiny of subjugation.
Receiver of seeds, willingly or unwillingly,
procreator of sons,
keeper of unnatural rhythms.

Ever since prehistoric times
Woman has struggled, resisted, defied, deserted,
endured, & transcended;
blossomed wildly, unexpectedly.
Even so,
Strong Woman has barely modified
time & history,
destiny & unnatural laws.

Ever since prehistoric times
Woman has been receiver of
instinctual wisdom,
compassionate giver of self,
mirror of daughters,
mother who nurtures &
encourages freedom, yet also
guards natural boundaries
with discernment & tenacity.

Ever since prehistoric times,
Woman has been sagacious, steadfast,
brave & compassionate
maiden, mother, grandmother,
matriarch, wise & empowered Crone,
no matter destiny,
no matter history,
no matter time & laws,

no matter the predators,
Strong Woman,
Immortal Woman
has prevailed.

I Must Unmask

To find meaning in my life,
I must unmask.
I know that,
but I'm afraid.
Afraid of not knowing what to do
with that embedded self,
afraid of creating chaos
in a seemingly orderly life.

The struggle is strong within,
I experience it in my bones,
a hidden self I must contend with
is trying to make sense,
wanting to surface,
afraid to emerge.

It is a lonely, painful unfolding,
yet powerful and instinctive.
It is a forceful yearning
which keeps me wanting to uncover,
to uncover the me who knows,
the one who is.

The process has begun,
there is no turning back.
Intuitive woman is resurrecting;
free, unconditional, intense, unfeigned,
vital woman is alive.
Come, I await you.
Come, I need embrace you.

Woman I Am

How do I describe myself?
How different am I today
from who I was yesterday?
I know I have changed,
everything changes,
nothing remains the same.
nothing is permanent.
Nonetheless,
I revel in my reality,
I am a woman.

A woman
who once was an infant
with curly, brown hair
and a great big pink bow
that insistently slid off.
Then, like magic,
I was a young child
who wore pink & white
dresses with frills & lace,
sewn with love by mother.

Almost too soon,
I became a young girl
who dreamt about love
but couldn't understand
how a stranger could
truly love her,
yet it happened.
In time I became a wife,
then a mother who
experienced the love of a man,
the love of her children &
the joys & pains that
accompany life's events.

Today, I am a woman
who has learned about
love's ups & downs,
how to be alone at times &
who values moments of happiness,
moments to celebrate,
no matter fears & doubts,
no matter losses & hurts.

I am a woman
who goes about the days
accomplishing her tasks,
yet also questioning
life & living,
death & departure,
her place in the universe,
even the will of God,
albeit, always believing
in His love.

Woman.
Woman.
Woman.
There is so much more to me
than gender.

I am
Love, Fear, Dependence,
Independence, Endurance,
Happiness, Kindness
Anger, Tears,
Frustrations,
Questions,
Vitality,
Resilience,
Spirituality.

I am
Nurturing
Trusting
Giving,
Evolving,
Woman
I am.

Idioma/**Language**

I think of words,
phrases, sentences,
exclamations!
Spanish/English
English/Spanish.
Mis idiomas/my languages,
my being/*mi ser.*
More than words,
phrases, or sentences,
language
is at the very core
of my existence.
Without language
my life would be
like a dam,
repressed
with thoughts,
emotions, wishes,
& dreams
unable to flow freely;
a prisoner
of my own self,
wanting to burst forth.

Language/*Idioma,*
more than words,
phrases, or sentences,
are my two worlds.
At times integrated,
separate when needed,
yet both permeating my life
with thoughts & emotions.
I dream in English
of a perfect world.
I make love in *español,*
mi amor, querido amor.
I write in English,

words flowing onto paper.
I cook in *español...*
ajo, cilantro, orégano,
herbs that have flavored
our foods for generations.

Language defines me,
language frees me,
language strengthens me.
*Mis idiomas/*my languages,
two languages,
two cultures,
one person.

Latina

Latina,
The island travels with you
wherever you go;
laughter,
vibrant colors,
warm smiles,
rich skin,
swaying hips.

Latina,
The island travels with you
wherever you go;
perpetual stereotypes,
harassment,
sexual innuendos,
menial jobs.

Hermanas Latinas,
this myth,
this old, pervasive myth
needs be overthrown,
transformation achieved,
belief in the power of self,
Educación,
Paciencia,
Persistencia,
Superación.

hermanas – sisters
educación education
persistencia – persistence
superación - overcome

Ser Madre

¿Saben?
Cuando era niña soñaba,
soñaba con ser madre.
Soñaba que mis hijos serían buenos e inteligentes,
soñaba que mis hijos serían obedientes,
y que me amarían mucho.
Un día, cuando ya no era niña,
llegó un joven a mi vida,
llegó el hombre que pensé sería el mejor padre,
y juntos soñamos.

Al pasar los años, llegaron esos hijos tan deseados,
uno muy bonito y sensible,
otro muy inteligente y querendón,
y aun otro muy alegre y saltarín.
¿Saben?
Aunque a veces se tornaban un tanto desafiantes,
o quizás hasta un poco engreídos,
todos fueron muy queridos,
todos fueron bienvenidos.
ellos hicieron mi sueño realidad,
ser madre.

Igual que yo, mis hijos crecieron,
soñaron sus propios sueños,
y se fueron a convertirlos en realidad.
Es la ley de la vida, según dicen.
Y hoy, después de tanto vivir,
después de tanto soñar,
estoy sola otra vez… pero....
¿Saben?
Sigo siendo madre.
No importa donde estén,
no importa con quien estén,
no importa si me llaman o no,
no importa si me visitan o no,
siguen siendo mis hijos.

Cada día que vivo, pienso en ellos.
Cada día que vivo, los amo más.
Cada día que vivo, hago oración por ellos.
Y así será siempre, todos los días,
hasta que esta mi vida terrenal culmine,
Madre, siempre seré madre.

To Be Strong

Over the ages,
the image of woman
as the weaker gender
has been perpetuated.
She needs protection,
they say,
she cannot do for herself,
they say,
she is unable to decide,
she needs to submit to man,
they say,
he is stronger.

What does it mean to be strong?
Does it mean physical strength?
Does it mean violence? Aggressiveness?
Does it mean to be devoid of emotions
as if wearing an invisible armor
that hides all feelings?

Woman, to be strong is to
withstand and overcome
the predicaments &
disappointments that life brings.
To be strong is to be
courageous and go forward
in spite of hostility or
intimidation.
To be strong is
not to allow misguided,
unfounded judgments
dictate your decisions or behavior.
To be strong is
not to accept the myth that you, woman,
are weak and powerless,
unable to make decisions,
unable to stand firm.

Woman,
recognize that you are strong.
You have great courage,
you are nurturing, giving,
intelligent & intuitive.
You are strong because you
love & have tolerance.
You are strong because
you have respect for others.
You are strong because
when you need to cry, you do,
and then continue going forward.
Woman,
know who you are,
respect yourself,
accept your strengths,
conquer unfounded fears,
stand tall.

The Woman in the Mirror

When I look in the mirror
I see a woman with
expressive, golden brown eyes,
fair skin, & enticing smile.
I see a wife & mother who
has so much love to give.
I also see a professional,
one who works hard &
is climbing the proverbial
corporate ladder.
Then I ask myself:
Why is it that in spite of all
my qualities & achievements,
there are times when thoughts
of unworthiness creep into
my mind and tell me that
I'm not good enough?

It is on those days that I
can only see a person who is
misunderstood, unloved & flawed.
The inner connection is broken,
the dense fog of unworthiness,
creeps in, holds on to me,
tight & unrelenting, causing
frustration, anxiety, inadequacy,
almost total breakdown.
The image of perfection
I try so hard to achieve fades,
self-judgment is harsh.

Then, like the miracle of nature
that dissipates early morning fog
through gentle, warm winds &
a sun that shines strong & unswerving,
the voices of self-criticism & censorship
are silenced.

I listen to my heart.
I choose to dwell on love & self-respect.
The fog lifts.
When I look in the mirror,
once again I see the woman I am,
courageous, grateful, persistent, loving.
I have imperfections, but they are
minimized when I accept them as
part of my humanity.
Once again I continue my quest
for a satisfying, well rounded life,
a life that is evolving.
Once again,
the woman in the mirror is well.

Looking Glass

Sometimes I see my world
through a glass, a glass of
Merlot, that is.
The world seems less complex,
sweeter & smoother,
even balanced.
Other times it's a glass of
Pinot Noir.
Those are the times
I feel a bit fickle,
thin skinned & susceptible,
especially susceptible to those
who inhabit my surroundings
by unwarranted association.
My entire existence pales and
seems washed out when
looking through this glass.

Now, truth be told,
the glass I enjoy the most
is the one with Cabernet Sauvignon,
from Bordeaux of course.
Its intensity, backbone and
notable structure infuses courage.
I especially enjoy the subtle,
almost imperceptible oak flavor
that causes me to feel strong &
capable of living my life.

Thus,
no matter my surroundings or
the winds of hurricane force or
the days of grey clouds,
I continue to stand tall, for
each day brings with it

a different glass, my looking glass,
which befittingly reconciles me
with the uncertain world I inhabit &
provides a distinctive,
uncommon, satisfying view.

2. LIFE EVOLVING

"Look around you. Everything changes. Everything on this earth is in a continuous state of evolving, refining, improving, adapting, enhancing...changing. You were not put on this earth to remain stagnant."

Steve Maraboli, <u>*Life, the Truth, and Being Free*</u>

The Path

From the moment we are born,
until we take our last breath,
we embark on an unpredictable journey
that takes us step by step from road to road,
through treacherous ups & downs,
around dark bends,
across peaceful plateaus.
Sometimes the way is pleasant & gratifying,
other times distressing, even painful,
but we continue walking.
Sometimes we move with determination,
perhaps driven by our dreams & expectations;
other times we move in fear & distrust
as we come upon paths that are obliged,
with no detours or returns in sight.
Helpless, we stand by, watching
as some of our dreams fall by the wayside,
requiring we reconfigure, change direction,
and begin anew.
It is then that we dare question the Cartographer,
we want to know why...why?...why?
There is no explanation.
Still, no matter our dreams and realities,
no matter the unexpected, or the disappointments,
deep within we find the will to continue on our way,
impelled by a force beyond our understanding.
Finally, we know.
We accept that till we breathe our last breath,
it is our path, ours alone,
no one else can walk it for us.

Revelation

Go ahead, write that poem,
wield words, conjure pictures,
paint your thoughts in vibrant colors,
open your eyes to that mythic self,
unmask your deepest passions.

Go ahead, write that poem,
ink those thoughts you hold within,
make explosions, purge your secrets,
make plain your confusions,
evoke tranquility.

Go ahead, write that poem,
dare to denude your veiled beliefs,
make sense of life, yours and mine,
liberate that imprisoned self,
taste the power of redemption.

Go ahead, write that poem,
you need to know you,
I need to know me.

Trees and Life

Trees are majestic creatures
whose roots dig deep into earth
in search of sustenance,
balance… life.
Above the ground their trunks,
over time,
grow wide & tall,
as if to flaunt strength
and claim
an honorable place in nature.
Its branches reach out into the sky,
seemingly in search of wisdom and,
as the seasons come & go,
they reflect the bareness
of necessary solitude,
only to be followed
by bursting green leaves
that proclaim the beauty of life.
And then, in time,
we witness with awe the synchronized
transformation of its leaves;
orange, yellow, and red leaves,
visible agents of change.

Oh magnificent trees that teach us
how at times our own lives
need be lived in necessary solitude,
with brief interludes of bountiful living,
followed by crucial, perhaps painful
passages of change,
of necessary death & renewal.
Only then can we,
from season to season,
dig deep within and
recalibrate our lives,
knowing that therein lies
our wisdom, honor, and strength.

Rain

Morning rises on cloudy skies,
Rain falls… falls…falls…
flows freely,
cleansing, purifying,
washing away unwanted decay,
washing away rootless impurities.
Lluvia cae...cae...cae...
pours on dry, parched ground
fortifying,
impelling creative forces,
growth and change.

Rain falls…falls…falls...
into my soul,
nostalgia surfaces,
memories of bygone loves,
regrets & sorrows,
unspoken words
well up &
        f l o w   a w a y.

Rain...rain...rain…
fall into my life,
wash away my indifference,
wash away my angers,
wash away my fears.
Lluvia suave, lluvia fresca,
fall...fall...fall...
into my soul,
permeate the obscure,
purge every corner,
help me rise
to face my destiny.

lluvia = rain cae = fall suave = soft fresca = fresh

Unbridled

Time flies.
A phrase I'm sure we say and often hear,
almost as if by saying it,
we can control its hurried pace,
adjust it to our speed, moods & quirks.
Yet deep within we know it's true,
time does not stand still,
time flies…unbridled,
and with it, we fly too.
Think about it.
We go through many changes,
reinvent old patterns & establish new ones.
It seems we are
always trying to keep up with time,
yet almost never getting ahead.

Time flies,
and with it, we continue moving
in our quest to discover, or perhaps
uncover new beginnings,
put closure on unwanted endings.
Think about it.
Maybe, just maybe, we could become
ageless & timeless explorers
who continue to dream &
ignore the should haves and what ifs.
Is it possible that we can find within
the strength to embrace new roles & visions,
to create a renewed self,
one who does not fear the threat of time?
Remember,
whether we dream new dreams or not,
whether we move on with passion or not,
one truth remains certain,
time flies…unbridled.

Awareness

Surrendering to our present circumstances
is not cowardice or conformity,
it is the realization that life is not perfect
and is always in movement.
Surrendering to our present circumstances
is to understand that at times
feeling sad or frustrated is
because we have delayed our dreams,
because we feel trapped by our
socially assigned obligations,
credos instilled in us at a tender age
that seem to constrain & limit.

Perhaps surrendering is not the right word
and in its place we need to say
awareness.
Awareness of our present moment
implies mindfulness & perseverance
fused with the knowledge
that life is not perfect,
that it is always in movement.
Awareness is knowing
that this, our present moment,
whether pleasant or disconcerting,
is not permanent.
Awareness is knowing that
the challenges & experiences lived
provide us with
direction & fulfillment and,
from time to time,
contentment.
Awareness is knowing and believing
we have nothing to regret because
life is not perfect and
is always in movement.

Life Lessons

I remember a song from long ago,
when I was a gullible thirteen year old.
It declared I had a destiny
that was my only happiness.
Back then it was one of my favorites.
Today, I ask,
Destiny? What is destiny?
What about free-will?
What about my ability and
right to make choices?

When I was young,
those thoughts did not concern me,
I lived a life I thought was free,
it didn't matter that I was part of
a larger, more powerful existence
governed by my parents.
Choices were made for me,
consequences shared or mitigated,
and in exchange, I felt safe.
I was an important piece,
or so I imagined,
of the puzzle called family

The years went by and at long last
I began to emerge out of my
protective shell of family,
cultural and gender boundaries,
risking the disapproval of my caretakers
and the warm comfort of home.
I realized that that which defined me,
in some ways also limited me.
I knew that the time had come,
I had to make my own way,
and so I did.

Today, as I take inventory,
I realize without doubt that
there will always be surprises,
good or bad.
I have learned that
even though I may not control
every twist and turn,
I still have a choice,
I can choose how to respond.
And so, I ask,
Is it destiny transcendent,
or is it unrivaled free-will?
I choose to believe that
life is a blending of both,
working and weaving
the way together, as one.
I am compelled to find and
accept my place
in this exciting, unpredictable,
at times inexplicable world,
while upholding a sense of self,
after all, it is my life.

Let Me Live

Dear conscience, be my guide,
not my prison guard.
Show me the way,
point out what is right,
what is wrong,
then step aside,
let me decide.
Let me take the risks of choices,
let me learn about consequences,
let me be me.

Dear conscience, don't
cause me to feel guilty,
I need to feel free,
to not worry or fear.
I need to trust myself,
to find a place
that appeases my quest,
perhaps somewhere
between right & wrong.

Dear conscience, I'm not
asking you to leave,
I'm asking you to walk beside me.
Prod me, but don't corral me;
be a gentle reminder,
respect my decisions,
I need to uncover my truth,
I need to live my life.

Backbone

Life is endlessly evolving.
We tread on territory
that at times seems
logical, anticipated, inevitable.
Yet there are times when life
is unexpected, daunting,
so confusing.
It is then that love,
only love,
makes those moments bearable,
even comprehensible.
Yes, love,
the backbone of life
that kindles courage,
will-power,
destination,
well-being.
It is the strong, constant,
unconditional love
that assures,
that gives meaning
and purpose to life.
In the end,
to sense, to know
that there is
one person, just one,
who makes evident
a love so deep
is to know that
life is good.

Sunset Promises

It is true that
I've experienced pain,
I've experienced suffering,
yet, it is also true that
even when those dark moments
seemed to defeat me,
I experienced love,
a love that has allowed me to
endure pain & sadness,
to live moments
of laughter & joy.

Yes, we all have had our share of
pain & suffering,
but in the midst of those experiences,
we need to step back
and contemplate the entire scene,
like when we admire a painting
by Van Gogh or Monet.
Breathtaking landscapes of sunsets
in yellow, red, and orange,
reminiscent of endings, of
letting go of our sadness, or
letting go of that we love
for the sake of survival.
Upon a closer look,
it seems that those well-known
paintings, in one way or another,
reflect a soft, diffused light,
somewhere...in the background,
a light that promises a new day,
perhaps brighter, happier,
a new beginning...sunrise.

And so it is that
no matter the dark foreboding clouds,
the red, menacing skies,
the descending orange sun,
there is always a soft light that prevails,
a light sustained by love & hope,
unwavering & unconditional.

Transition

Transition.
A word that compels us to meditate
on how we have journeyed through life;
from one stage to another,
from one path to another,
sometimes serenely,
other times in turbulence;
sometimes unconsciously,
other times with mindfulness.

Transition.
The metamorphosis of those who
go forward with great expectations
and courage on a journey that
at times is so demanding.
It is the progression of those
who are sustained by a force
that is greater than theirs.
It is the movement of those who
decidedly re-examine old ways,
push boundaries,
create new patterns,
thereby opening doors
to greater experiences & changes,
understanding that life's transitions
will challenge ingrained notions
as well as provide an
interconnectedness with unforeseen,
unknown dimensions.

Transition.
A word that impels us to move on,
knowing that the new & unfamiliar
way that lies before us
needs to be walked
with strength & determination;

knowing that nothing lasts forever
and that our lives,
from beginning to end,
will always be in transition.

Forgiveness

To forgive is to let go,
let go of an offense, a betrayal,
hurtful words & actions
thrown at me by another,
sometimes trusted,
considered a friend,
perhaps even loved.

To forgive is to let go,
let go of the pain another has caused
without provocation, without reason,
making it so much more difficult
because I cannot understand why,
why is that person
so hateful, so heartless.

To forgive is to let go & understand
that holding on to an offense
hurts and causes me
to feel sad & bitter,
perhaps even unworthy.

To forgive is to let go & understand
I cannot change the offender.
Rather, I need to go deep inside
and mend my lacerated heart.
I need to wash away
any lingering feelings of
anger, indignation, or revenge.

To forgive is to let go & know
that everything has an end...
words, feelings...even others.
To forgive & let go is
to find peace within.

Want Ad, Unclassified

Wanted!
Someone who is friendly,
and compassionate,
who likes to talk.

Wanted!
Someone who has
contagious gladness &
is able to make me smile,
even if I don't feel like it.

Wanted!
Someone who listens
to what I have to say &
then hugs me in response,
even if he doesn't agree,
or understand.

Wanted!
Someone who will sit by me &
hold me when I am sad,
no questions asked,
no explanations required.

Wanted!
Someone who will share with me
his love of life,
his fresh and uplifting thoughts
on that which weighs me down.

Wanted! Wanted! Wanted!
Someone to walk with me on
this unknown, adventurous &
sometimes treacherous
road called life.

Most important,
that someone must be willing
to hold my hand &
never let go.

Enlightenment

Lightning struck!
Unbound
by high voltage,
I'm learning to love myself,
finding my voice
in an energized,
mood lifting
euphoria
never before experienced.
Inferiority complex,
mind clutter & unwarranted fears
lobotomized
(lightning has been known to do that).
Now I know,
I finally know,
it's so clear.
There are no right answers,
just life, my unique life;
at times imploding
or even exploding,
but most important,
always evolving,
transcending.

3. RELATIONSHIPS...
UNTANGLING

"We all strive for balance, often moving to extremes to find ourselves somewhere in the middle where we can sustainably exist in optimal inspiration. Working toward balance takes a lot of ingredients. We need courage, reflection, attention, action, and a push-and-pull relationship between effort and relaxation"

Tara Stile

White Elephant

A white elephant,
mystical sign
of good luck,
peace & prosperity,
seemingly brings sorrow to
the lovers who can't
make up their minds
on what to keep,
what to discard.
This indecision,
or perhaps fear,
causes shadows to creep in
here and there,
casting darkness over
what once was passionate,
& exhilarating.

A white elephant,
mythical symbol
of unwanted possessions
that have become a burden,
difficult to get rid of,
makes its triumphant
entrance into the lives of
two lovers who seemed
so close, so connected,
yet now choosing to travel
parallel roads, where,
as far as the eye can see,
there are no trees,
no shade,

both understanding too well
that what once was theirs,
so rare, so venerated,
will never be theirs again.

I Know Him

When I look at him today,
I see a strange man
in a frail, tired body,
who over and over
wrings his hands.
He looks at me
with empty eyes
and asks who I am.
He's not a stranger.
I know him.
I know his likes & dislikes,
I know what his dreams were
and what heights he reached.
I was there.
Yes, I know him, but
his eyes tell me he's not there,
he doesn't know me,
he's gone.

His empty look provokes regret
of all the moments I wanted to say
I love you, but let them go by,
moments that can't be undone,
that cause a hounding guilt
and profound sadness because
after so many years of
enjoying each other, of
embracing each other's differences,
of letting go or holding tight,
today, he doesn't know who I am.
Nonetheless,
it doesn't matter.
I remember.
I know him.
I still love him.
So I smile, take his hand in mine
and whisper my name in his ear
one more time.

Broken Promises, Broken Ties

This so-called amicable breakup
was a long time coming.
Our busy schedules allowed us no time
for sitting together in the evenings
to talk, read, watch TV, or
simply sip some wine and relax.
No time for kisses, hugs, much less
whispered sweet nothings.
We were always too tired to go out
for dinner or a movie together,
not even once a week.
Too tired for this, too tired for that,
even too tired to make love,
always too tired.

I didn't say out loud how hurt and
angry I was for fear of becoming a nag.
He did not like confrontations,
for years we kept up appearances,
we both remained silent.
The silence was a mask.
Inside me the words kept
pushing & pulling & piling up,
creating volcanic rumblings
on the brink of eruption.
To my surprise, or perhaps not,
it happened one day.
The pent up words erupted and
flowed hot and fiery,
like molten lava flows
down the side of a mountain.
The words burned my throat,
but I managed to say them
while experiencing nervousness,
disappointment, sadness,
frustration, anger & fear.

I told him I wanted more, more
than what he seemed willing to give.
If he did not want to consider change,
I was willing to leave.
I was willing to leave behind
our history together, our friends & family,
even our house and its contents.
His only question was:
Are you sure?
No anger, no defense, no willingness
to openly discuss my claims,
no desire to validate our love,
no desire to validate the years
we had been together.

That's why I left.
In spite of my fears & sadness,
in spite of my disillusion,
in spite of loving him,
I left.

Phone Call

The phone rang insistently.
She answered.
A voice from the past reverberated,
rupturing her peace.
Forgive me,
he begged.
I was confused,
Didn't know what I was saying,
didn't mean to hurt you.
Please,
take me back,
I need you,
I need your comfort.

Confused?
Didn't know what you were saying?
You seemed so sure,
so adamant.
Your words whipped me.
Every fiber of my body was hurting.
My spirit mourned the deadly blows
for days and months.

Forgive me,
he cried out again.
I discovered I still love you.
I was blinded momentarily,
foolishly trying to regain youth,
not valuing our love.
I need you,
I need your knowing ways.

My knowing ways?
You forced me to learn about loneliness,
you forced me to learn that love dies,
you forced me to learn that life continues.
So, I learned.

I learned to heal my wounds,
I learned to live for myself,
I even learned to laugh & love again.

Forgive you?
I forgave you that day I looked in the mirror
and discovered a different woman.
She's vibrant.
She's happy.
She's strong.
That woman you left found a new path,
her path and only hers.
She doesn't need you to define her anymore.
Ciao, she whispered softly &
ended the phone call.

Life, Love & Time

I was young when we met,
somewhat naive,
not knowing about life
and its ups and downs,
only wanting to know love.
He was young too,
not so naive,
life for him had been
more demanding.
more difficult.
We married and began
our life, a new life, a good life.
Together we made plans
and strived to make them
our reality.
Together we loved, cried,
laughed, worked,
argued, made-up, and then
loved some more.

Time and happenings
caused us to mature,
to be more knowing
of our surroundings,
of each other,
of our likes & dislikes,
of our joys & sorrows;
we were not so naive anymore.
We learned how to continue loving
in the midst of all the
doings & undoings of life,
some days less,
most days more.

Today I'm not so young,
I know a bit more about life & love,
the sacrifices & rewards,

the disappointments,
the satisfactions,
the companionship.
Most of all,
I am glad to have met him,
I am glad to have loved him.
With him, my life
has been so much better.

Tell Me

I need to know, tell me,
Do you love me?
Pay attention, come,
sit down here, next to me,
listen to my dreams,
share in my frustrations,
feel my anger,
wipe away my tears,
touch me
in a deep, discerning way,
I need to know.
Tell me with words you know so well,
tell me how much you love me.
It's not enough that you
go out to work for me,
as you say.
It's not enough that you
come home each night to me.
I hunger for your words,
I need to feel you say the words,
I need to see you say the words.
Come, look into my eyes,
tell me how much you love me,
tell me how much you need me,
take me in your arms,
whirl me round & round,
dance me to the moon.
I need to know.....
          I need to know.

Perhaps Then

I begged the universe
to allow me to surrender
to your love proclaimed,
to your promises of bliss
that are alluring
and cause me to sense
the me who is,
the me who hides,
broken and
in fear of being hurt again,
abandoned.
I cried out to the universe
to allow me to accept
your displays of devotion
and apparent truthfulness
of your words, but
the universe did not respond.
Or did it?
Perhaps its silence
was telling me to
rely on my instincts,
to take risks,
to trust the clarity and power
of your intentions.
Perhaps then I'll be able to
take in all that love
you claim to feel for me.
Perhaps then I will
experience a different
passion,
calm and profound.
Perhaps then this
gnawing emptiness
and fear that cripples
will go away.

A Life Worth Living

Sometimes she hid
behind large dark glasses
or wore floppy hats &
sweaters, even if it was hot.
She tried to hide
the black & blues,
the cuts & bruises
from her neighbors' meddling eyes &
her family's accusatory questions
until one day,
fear of imminent death forced her
to flee her home, young ones in tow.

For months she had planned,
scrimped & saved for
this decisive moment,
but she waited & waited,
perhaps believing his lies of change,
of never again, of I love you,
only to feel his inebriated fists and kicks
again & again on her body, on her soul.
Now she was convinced.
He will not change.
It will never happen.

Without warning or announcement,
without looking back,
she left on a cold Monday morning.
She left her beautiful house and
all it contained repeating over & over,
I will keep going, I need to survive,
there has to be a better life.
And so began a parade of motels,
dirty & dingy cheap motels,
almost as bad as staying home
with him, she thought once,
but her mantra kept her going,

she had to endure,
for herself and her babies.

She struggled to find a job,
sufficient pay for child care,
food & safe harbor.
She bounced from job to job,
from motel to motel,
till one fateful day a helping hand
reached out to her.
The safe harbor home became
her refuge;
her children were safe,
she was safe.
Through kindness, understanding,
determination & time,
her wounds began to heal.
She took back control of her life,
she no longer blamed herself,
she uncovered and reconstructed
her battered self-worth.
Above all, she was able to
let go of him & her past.
She dared to visualize a better life,
it was a life of hard work,
nonetheless, a life filled with
peace & love & satisfaction,
a life worth living.

4. REALITY SHIFTING

"As you are shifting, you will begin to realize that you are not the same person you used to be. The things you used to tolerate have become intolerable. When you once remained quiet, you are now speaking your truth. Where you once battled and argued, you are now choosing to remain silent. You are beginning to understand the value of your voice and there are some situations that no longer deserve your time, energy, and focus."

The Minds Journal

Driftwood

There are days when I experience
an unexpected feeling of sadness
that overpowers the beauty and
excitement of a new day.
I do not plan those moments,
they just happen and bring with them
a despondency that seems to emerge
from a place deep inside that causes me
to be silent and retreat
from the presence of others.
I want no conversations,
no need to explain myself or
answer questions for which
I have no responses.
I want to be in solitude, in deep thought,
so I can search within my mind's maze
to find a cause, a logical reason
for this unprovoked sadness.
I allow the feeling to exist,
to move from here to there,
and then, once more,
I uncover my truth.
Sweet & sad memories I thought
securely hidden from sight & mind
have emerged, like driftwood that is
moved by the winds and tides
of time and events, then,
washed ashore
where it becomes visible, palpable.
Sometimes, driftwood is collected
and given new life.
Other times, the tides return it to
the deep blue sea where
winds & waves move it from side to side
till it is no longer visible on the horizon.

Perhaps one day my driftwood will
be taken by the tides, winds, and waves
farther and farther into the deep blue sea
and never return.
Perhaps.

I Am My Father's Daughter

On occasion,
my husband tells me that
I am my father's daughter,
and even though I perceive
an undertone of reproach,
I thank him because
so many times before,
that nostalgic thought
has come to mind.
There are things I do,
actions I take
that speak my father's name.
Among them,
my love of books, pens &
beautiful writing
all evoke his presence.
My perseverant pursuit of issues
that threaten deep-rooted principles,
I learned from him.
I am my father's daughter,
a thought that makes me glad,
even though at times
it causes me to be sad,
for I know there will never be
a son or daughter who
will smile and say,
I am my mother's child.

My Inner Child

My inner child is always present.
Sometimes she's quiet and
sits in a remote, dark corner
trying not to cause trouble,
keeping out of the way.
Other times she wants to come out
and run, play, and laugh;
she wants to feel free,
do whatever makes her happy,
without restriction,
like when she colors.
My inner child loves to color,
especially with brand new crayons;
oh the soothing aroma of new crayons!
She colors up-and-down and
side-to-side; red, yellow green!
So much fun,
no cares, no worries.

But, as usual,
in the midst of all that fun,
the adult steps in and
questions the worthiness of
what she calls nonsensical,
inappropriate behavior.
A waste of time!
My inner child cringes,
and once again retreats
into her remote, dark corner,
and waits, waits; she
waits for another chance
to come out and play.

My inner child does not give up.
She will try again, and hopes
maybe next time the adult will
understand that once in a while,

albeit for a short while,
her sweet, loving, care-free
inner child needs to take over
the regimented, dull & at times
depressing adult life and
do whatever helps put aside
the angers, fears, and worries
that overwhelm.
My inner child knows that
if she is freed to come out,
it could be a life-saving moment.

Dreaming and Waiting

So many times I've considered
changing my life
just to escape the present.
Perhaps it's the glitches
of a long day,
of anxiety caused by people,
moments & boundaries
that will not change anytime soon.
Perhaps I try too hard to
walk ahead of the storm,
dreaming of a new life,
lived with lights on &
straight talk,
no loaded silences,
no time-worn secrets,
no closed doors.
Soon the dream ends &
here I am,
eyes wide open,
living my long days,
biding my time,
waiting,
      …waiting.

Hidden Anguish

Sometimes, only sometimes,
my arms ache from the need
to hold a child,
not any child, my child.
I need to hold her
close & secure next to my heart
so I can breathe in
the sweet aroma of innocence,
and feel the softness of
her small, tender body.

Sometimes, only sometimes,
my body & soul hunger to hold
in my lonely arms
the young child that once was,
and then bury my nose in her
neck so I can take in the
intoxicating elixir of purity,
love, and radiant warmth
that infuses life into every
corner of my existence.

Sometimes, only sometimes,
I am strong enough to silence
my aches and innermost desires
for the palpable love of my child.
I am able to hide those
feelings that emerge from
the depths within,
feelings that refuse to die,
feelings that I know will rise again,
time & place unknown.

Empty Nest

Once upon a time,
this big ole house was bursting with life.
My kids were always playing, hollering, crying,
silence was a rarity, neatness unheard of.
Sometimes I scolded or punished them,
other times I laughed and joined them.

The days, months & years went by
as if on roller derby skates.
The kids grew up & went away.
Too soon, I thought,
this big ole' house was empty, quiet,
only the echoes of laughter and
shrilly voices remained.
Some days I walk from room to room,
perhaps hoping to find my babies,
but I'm greeted by deafening silence,
an emptiness that hurts.

Now, from time to time, I must say,
my kids return
with their own offspring in tow and
this big ole' house shudders & awakens to
screaming & hollering that seems to
ricochet off its happy walls.
The empty echoes fade,
the bedrooms are messy,
the kitchen bustles with activity;
a half-eaten sandwich is on the counter,
the coffee pot is brewing and
the dishwasher is humming its happy song.

There is warmth, there is love,
there is life
in this big ole house again.
But, time does not stand still,
it continues its relentless path and,

too soon the silence returns,
too soon I find myself walking
a worn, familiar path
from room to room,
listening to the new echoes and
waiting, waiting.
Together we wait,
we wait for their return,
this big ole house and me.

Daydreaming

On my better days,
I love the window over my kitchen sink,
from where I can watch
the going and coming of neighbors, their
kids running and screaming, having fun;
it takes my mind off the mundane task
of washing cups and dishes,
scrubbing pots and pans.

Then, there are the other days when
I hate the window over my kitchen sink
and wished it was a brick wall instead.
Those are the days my mind wanders
and enters the mystifying
paths of the imagination.
Those are they days I see my own kids,
unbiddenly gone before me.

As if by magic,
I see my first born, twelve years old,
sitting on the porch across the street with her friend.
I'm sure they are talking about boys.
Sometimes they whisper, other times they laugh.
I remember when I was twelve.

My second daughter is ten,
she's somewhat of a tomboy.
I see her riding her bike with the boys next door.
There she goes,
screeching and racing, vying for first place.

Then there's my youngest,
a healthy, robust boy who plays on
the neighborhood Little League Team.
I see him coming home, face grimy & sweaty,
uniform covered with mud

from stealing bases to win the game.
What a rascal!

Suddenly,
a cup slips out of my hands and
crashes into the sink!
As it breaks into a thousand tiny pieces,
my wandering mind comes back,
back to my reality of
a house without children,
a house that is quiet & tidy,
a house that is painfully barren,
a house with a window over the kitchen sink.

New Mother

Oh new mother, young professional
Whose long hours, days, and years of studies
have been rewarded.
Oh young, hardworking executive
who generously contributes to the household budget:
new mortgage, new car, college loans, hospital bills,
daycare, credit cards, and more.

Oh dear mother, newly minted young mother,
filled with love and remorse,
shrouded in sadness, imbued with anger
when each morning you scoop up your child,
precious bundle, and deliver her to strangers' care.

Oh vibrant mother, well prepared professional,
yet so unprepared as absent mother.
Every morning the floodgates of guilt open and
you drown in self-reproach and doubt,
only to have that burden lifted every evening
when your smiling little one is in your arms.

Oh young mother, ambitious executive
learning how to balance life,
trying hard to rid yourself of feelings of
misdoing and selfishness,
a difficult task when in the presence of
innocent tears.

Dear devoted mother,
don't let remorse assail you,
be kind to yourself,
your child will thrive,
your love will suffice,
your love will transcend.

My Secret World

There is a world,
somewhere deep within me,
where I am safe,
where there are no fears,
no misinterpretations,
no manipulations,
where I am me.

There is a world,
somewhere deep within me,
far from my reality,
where the impossible is possible,
where I am not young or old,
just me,
ageless & vibrant.

In that world, that secret world,
I need not worry
if I am good enough, smart enough,
or even pretty enough.
It is a place without concerns
about who likes me, or even
who loves me.

In that world, my secret world,
I find peace & tranquility,
the shackles of must do and
must be, magically disappear,
allowing me to be that person
I know is there,
deep inside of me,
at times strong & confident,
at times insecure,
easily broken.

There is a world,
somewhere deep inside of me
that allows me, from time to time,
to escape my reality.
a place where I can accept
my vulnerabilities without guilt
and for a fleeting moment,
I am simply me,
uncomplicated & content.
I am free.

Dare

Letting go of the past
is a brave, solitary act
because at times painful memories
seem to validate our present existence;
they keep us fearing, hating, sighing...crying.

Letting go of unfulfilled dreams
is as agonizing as fulfillment itself,
for we seem to believe that by holding on,
our hurt will somehow be alleviated.

Letting go of stifling lives,
commitments no one seems to value,
that cause fatigue and turn out empty,
may seem like an assault on domesticity.

Letting go of burdens so heavy
they make us weak, make us question
our intellect, our intuition, or
cause inertia, even humiliation,
is so overwhelming.

Dare we let go and make room
for new dreams, new lives?
Dare we let go and free that trapped spirit
that desires to soar higher and higher?
Dare we let go and forge new memories?
Dare we?
    We must...
           we must let go...
                   just let go!

It's Time

I've been told by many to embrace life,
that I have the power to
live my life the way I want it to be,
not what others say it should be.
Again and again I have felt
confused, sad & fictitious,
leading a life that is often
empty and lonely.
It's over.
The time has come to hang the
"Do Not Disturb" sign
on the doorknob of my heart
for everyone to see.
It's time to discard the so-called
Master Plan of my life
and concoct a surprise about-face.
It's time to remove those leeches
who try to siphon the little joy I have
by making me feel guilty
for what is out of my control.
It's time to let those others meet
the genuine me who has been hiding
behind the curtain of falsehood
in pursuit of acceptance.
It's time to meet the me who will
try hard to embrace the ups and downs
of life and move on,
perhaps slowly and in a direction that is
not to everyone's liking,
but nonetheless, moving on.
It's time.

Pondering Life

When I think of my life and where I am today,
the thought that goes round & round is
that life seems to be slipping away and
there is no return.
Where have all the years gone?
A well-known phrase becomes a mantra,
It seems like only yesterday...
I was young and energetic;
I was studying, working, loving my life,
keeping in tune with the rhythms &
flows of life, yet through it all,
things changed,
sometimes at will, other times unwillingly.
Life experiences, new relationships,
unfamiliar surroundings,
birth & death,
have all provoked changes.

Births are happy moments,
they bring with them
the promise of immortality,
renewed youth, hopes & dreams.
Loss of a loved one brings sadness &
searing thoughts about life when
faced with the reality that
everything the beloved embodied
will be forgotten over time.
The same way photos fade,
memories fade and disappear.

Thus, here I am today,
approaching the end of my life &
still pondering the meaning of life,
the brevity of life, and wondering
if love is the key to longevity,
not a physical span of time,
but a spiritual one.

Perhaps to love profoundly
and be loved
may be the answer.
Perhaps we will live in
the hearts of those we loved
as long as they shall live.
Perhaps.

She's The One

For so long I've had to travel miles
before I can be with her, too long, I might add.
But, here I am tonight,
I am home.
I sit at the kitchen table and watch her
brewing a cup of steaming *café con leche*
and chatting about family, who visited, who didn't;
on and on she drones while I just sit and watch.

I see her hands which once were silky smooth,
now wrinkled and spotted,
yet deftly moving from here to there
concocting that heavenly brew.
Her hair is greying fast, too fast I think,
since now she refuses to color it.
Her round, expressive eyes reveal
the sadness and frustrations of life's surprises.

On impulse I go to her and put my arms
around her soft body and
hold her close, hold her tight,
like I know she held me long ago.
She laughs…I smile
and desperately hold back the tears
for all the years I've not been there,
not held her.

I release my hold and look at her again,
this time I see the woman who loved me
from the very first moment she knew I existed;
the one who brought me into this world;
the one who rocked me to sleep and sang,
Duerme mi niña, duérmete ya.
I see the one who first whispered love words
in my ears…*Te amo hija.*
The one who stayed up nights and cried
because I was sick;

the one who sewed frilly dresses and
hid Christmas gifts from my curiosity;
the one who was always waiting
when I got back from school.
I see the one who said she wouldn't
cry at my wedding, but did anyway.

The coffee's ready, we sit at the table…
slowly sipping the warm, soothing brew
and rekindling our memories.
Today she's here and I am home.
Tomorrow?
Tomorrow is too far away.

café con leche - latte
Duerme mi niña, duerme ya – sleep my child, sleep now
Te amo, hija – I love you daughter

What is Love?

What did I know about love
when I was young and so naive?
I believed in fairy tales
and princes on white horses,
and castles on hillsides,
and happy-ever-afters.
What did I know
that life could hurt so much?
That life is not perfect,
that some joys bring pain,
that giving can cause
an emptiness so profound
it seems impossible to fill?
But I learned.
Life taught me through
disappointments,
pain, and tears.
I learned about
the risks of love,
I learned about the
sacrifices of love.
I learned that love
needs the kiln of life
with its high temperatures
and flames that purify
disappointments,
pain and tears
until they are but old scars
that one can bear.
I learned that the love
which survives
trials and imperfections
provides the strength and
courage needed
to laugh and
be happy again.

For You

This poem is for you,
for the years shared,
in love & happiness,
in anguish and angers,
always together.
This poem is for the strong bond
that the years have forged
between you and me,
allowing us to depend on
one another,
yet also allowing us the freedom
to be unique individuals
with our own ideas & illusions,
a freedom that only those
who love can experience.
This poem is for you,
in memory of that young man
I once knew,
full of energy, decided, tenacious,
yet also tender and passionate.

This poem is for you,
the man you are today,
somewhat serene & subdued,
yet still determined and strong.
This poem is for the man
who day by day shows me
in so many ways
a love transformed,
rooted in countless moments lived,
a love that only time
can nurture & develop.
This poem is for you,
the man I have loved, love, and
will always love.
This poem is for you,
my husband.

5. DEATH AND DEPARTING

"Serenity is the balance between good and bad, life and death, horrors and pleasures. Life is, as it were, defined by death. If there wasn't death of things, then there wouldn't be any life to celebrate."

Norman Davies

The Angels Came

The day the angels came
was a fine summer day;
the sun shone bright,
the sky seemed bluer than ever before,
the billowy clouds danced to & fro.
The day the angels came,
I was not altogether surprised,
I knew deep down inside
that one day they would come,
even though I wished & prayed they would not.
The day the angels came
became for me a cold & bitter day,
a day of darkness, a day of agony & despair,
for on that day, on that fateful day,
my own sweet angel-child was taken from me,
away, far away to her celestial home.
Yes, I remember it well,
it was on that day,
the day the angels came.

My Plea

Dear God,
Are you there?
Are you listening to me?
Hear my prayer.
I need you to make my child well.
Please,
don't let him die.

Dear God,
I want my child by my side.
I want to read him bedtimes stories.
I want to see him ride a bike and
run around screaming & hollering
with other kids just like him.
I want to see him go off to kindergarten,
first grade, and then keep on going
all the way through college.
I want to hear him hound me for my car
when he gets his driver's license.
I want to lose sleep over him
when he's late getting home.
I want to see him tackle his first job.
I want to hear him say, "I love you, Mom."
I even want to hear his angers & disagreements.
I want to watch him fall in love & marry,
though it means he will go away.
I want to see my grandchildren.
I want to see how the life that began inside of me
evolves & blossoms fully into a life that is free,
yet somehow reflects a part of me.

Dear God,
Are you there?
Hear my cry.
Please,
Don't let him die.
Don't deny us
our life together.

Immortality

There is an emptiness
deep, deep. down
inside of me
that no one,
no thing,
no belief
can ever fill.
It is that space
my first born child filled,
deep, deep, down
inside of me.
it is that space
where she was formed,
it is that space
where she evolved,
so mysteriously, so securely,
so wonderfully.
it is that space
my firstborn child left
the day she emerged
into this world.
That day was one
that celebrated love and life,
a day in which fear and pain
magically faded when this,
my firstborn child,
was snugly placed
in my warm and loving arms.
Oh round, cherubic face,
Oh soft, curly hair,
I looked at her and saw myself,
she was my immortality.
Many a night I dreamt
of how our lives would be,
of love, of joy,
of giving, of receiving,
and yes, of angers and

frustrations too.
Yet those envisionments
remained just that,
futile dreams
of what might have been,
dreams denied me by fate,
if you wish,
and in their place remains
an eternal emptiness,
deep, deep, down
inside of me
that no one,

no thing

no belief

can ever,

ever fill.

Our Song of Love

When I am dead, my dearest,
sing a song of love for me,
plant daisies & sunflowers galore
till they fill the meadow
by our home and then,
every time you look at them,
hum our song of love.
Please do not be sad, but rather,
smile and remember me.
I will be the rain
coaxing the flowers to grow,
I will be the sun,
causing them to bloom,
I will be the wind,
dancing to and fro.
If you do this, my dearest,
I promise you,
our song of love will never die.

No Goodbyes

You left without a warning,
so quickly, quietly,
bewildering to me.
There was no time to talk,
no time to comprehend,
no time to say goodbye.

So many times before,
we laughed, we cried,
talked seriously or jokingly
about that hounding final moment
which came so furtively,
no time to say goodbye.

Perhaps your peaceful, sudden flight
was just the way you wanted;
perhaps you sensed goodbyes to be
enduring and decisive, so,
we need not say goodbye.

You left without a warning,
you went ahead of me.
Someday I know I'll see you,
we'll talk and laugh again.
At last I understand, my love,
no need to say goodbye.

"Where, oh Death, is Your Victory?" *

Be it known that
only love owes no dues to death.
Be it known that
those who love,
those who are brave in the midst of adversities,
those who are kind, even in the face of callousness,
those who are loyal to themselves and to others
have set a foundation that defies death and oblivion.
Death is not their enemy,
Death does not distress them,
nor does it cause fear or trepidation in their hearts.
Be it known that
those who love and are loved
never die.
"Where, oh death, is your sting?" *

*I Corinthians 15:55

Who?

Who will remember me when I'm gone?
Who will remember
my warm smile and spontaneous laughter,
or my large and probing eyes?
Who will remember
that I cried at the movies
whether the ending was happy or sad,
knowing that I cried for a life so inscrutable,
for a world so perplexing?
Who will remember
my love of books,
my hunger for learning, for understanding
the intricacies of our humanness,
my quest for a place in the universe?
Who will remember
how profoundly I loved my family,
how sincerely I loved my friends,
how intensely I loved a man,
how eternally I loved my children?
Who will remember
my loneliness in the midst of a crowd?
Who will remember
that melancholic, forlorn self
that sporadically surfaced,
in spite of others, in spite of myself?
I ask again and again,
Who?
    Who
        will
            remember
                me
                  when
                    I'm gone?

Legacy

You are gone!
Just like that!
Quietly, serenely, decisively,
knowing your destination.

So many times before
during your long,
drawn out illness,
we thought about it,
spoke about it,
imagined it,
but now it's done.
You are gone.
The piercing pain of loss
breaks our spirit.

It is done.
You are gone.
But…then again,
not completely.
A part of you lives on
in each one of us.
You are present
in that discerning smile,
unfaltering walk,
and persuasive talk.
You are present
in how we view life,
in how we live life,
in how we share life.
Yes….for many,
you are gone,
but not for us.
The essence of who you were
remains.

That's your legacy.
How comforting to know,
Dad,
you are still with us.

Mother

For days and hours I sat next to Mother's
hospital bed watching her breathe.
At times I touched her forehead,
her hands, so warm, yet,
with each breath she took,
the end of her life was approaching.

I remembered she would tell stories
of growing up on a farm
along with many brothers and sisters.
As the eldest, she helped care for them;
She did what she could,
given the circumstances.

Once she told me she learned how to
cook at a very young age,
so young that she had to stand on a
wooden crate to reach the large,
hot pots filled with boiling water and
vianda, tubers that were staples at
the dinner table.

Most of their clothes were handmade,
so she learned how to sew and did it well.
She also learned how to embroider
handkerchiefs to help her mother
earn extra money for store-bought necessities
like kerosene for the lamps, or shoes
for the young ones to wear
when they walked to school.
Mother did what she could,
given the circumstances.

As the young and beautiful girl that
she was with large brown eyes
and long wavy dark hair,
she fell in love with a handsome

neighboring fellow, but soon
it became a forbidden love.
He is a womanizer, they said,
he will make you unhappy, they said.
And so, though heartbroken, she left him.
She did what was expected of her,
given the circumstances.

Soon after and not very willingly,
she left her family at the farm and
arrived in Brooklyn. They said it was
to help provide for them, but
she knew it was to establish distance
between her and her first love,
to help her forget,
something I know is not always possible.

Then, months after her arrival and
because life insists on moving along,
she was introduced to another young man,
one who met with family approval.
She was advised and prodded
into a marriage with the one
she did not love.
I suppose she did what was expected,
given the circumstances.

Over the years and perhaps to her surprise,
she discovered her husband truly was
a good man, a God-fearing man who
was kind, generous, and even loving.
She accepted her role as wife and mother,
perhaps at times in a not so pleasant manner,
but she did the best she could,
given her circumstances.

As I contemplate her today,
slowly slipping away,
what I know and remember
about her life comes to mind
and I can't help but wonder,
was she ever happy?
You know, those fleeting moments
of pure joy and well-being we
experience when we share our lives
with those we love.
Did she ever feel loved?
Did she?
I hope she did.

6. REMINISCING AND RECONCILING

"I've never tried to block out the memories of the past, even though some are painful. I don't understand people who hide from their past. Everything you live through helps to make you the person you are now."

Sophia Loren

Looking Back

In my quest to understand my present moment,
and perhaps to find a better path,
from time to time,
I look back.

Once, when I looked back to my childhood,
I recalled the many ways my life was steered
with rigid ideas and beliefs
that served to define who I was,
what was expected of me and how,
as the firstborn,
I had to be a role model.
I tried my best to please,
to make mine the beliefs and strict,
narrow precepts that were handed down.
I remember I was always looking for
approval, complements on my
submissive & well-orchestrated behavior.
Such actions & words were sparse, almost absent.
Hence, I grew up trying to please everyone,
 waiting for approval, complements.
So many times, in their absence,
I felt insecure, sad, even discouraged,
like the child of years ago.

That fateful moment I looked back,
I realized I needed to rid myself
of this emotional baggage.
I needed to make room for who I am today.
I needed to believe in myself,
with all my virtues & imperfections
because that is the authentic me.
I do not need to be validated by others,
I know my worth.

And so, in my quest to understand
my present moment,
I know that from time to time
it's good, perhaps almost necessary,
to look back.

Carousel Horse

Oh, how I would love to ride
a carousel horse again
like I did when I was a child.
Not just any horse, though,
I want to ride the white one
with the royal blue bridle
and flaming red saddle.
That's the one that seemed to gallop high
as it went round & round and up & down,
taking me away on an unforgettable adventure
that had no beginning and no end.
Some riders would reach out trying to snag
the brass ring to get a free ride,
but others, like me, didn't care,
all we wanted was to feel
the wind hitting our faces,
our hair flying wildly like manes;
it was energizing, exhilarating, liberating.
There were no worries, no frustrations
or disappointments to hold us back.
When we rode the carousel horses
we were galloping away, away, away,
feeling free & invincible in our innocence.
The world beyond was a whirling blur
that did not matter or cause concern.
Oh to ride that carousel horse again,
to feel free & indomitable,
even if only for a brief moment,
even if only in my dreams.

Slamming Doors

I was fourteen, I was in love,
at least I thought I was.
But my love was forbidden,
a la Romeo & Juliette.
"Too young, so naive,"
Dad would say.
"You don't govern yourself,"
Mom would say.
But still my heart beat faster
each time I saw him,
my first love.

Frustrations, thoughts of a life unfair
cluttered my mind.
I felt my powerlessness,
but dared not talk back,
that is, until one day,
frustrations running high,
feeling disrespected, misunderstood,
I marched to my room and
slammed the door,
slammed hard,
slammed real hard,
almost off its hinges hard.
Such power!
Such show of force!
Such defiance!
I even scared myself, but felt oh, so good.
A mystery to me my parents let me live.

Today I don't slam doors as much,
but have been known to slam a few.
Perhaps I need to show who I am,
make clear my stance,
demand respect.

And so, I vouch to you, my friend,
that feeling of powerlessness
that sometimes wants to emerge
is momentarily mitigated
by simply slamming a door.
But remember,
make sure to slam hard,
slam real hard,
almost off its hinges hard!

Sometimes

It's good to be alone sometimes
and have a nook where I can
think and think again.
To have time to make decisions,
time to provide awaited answers,
time to forgive,
time to forget.

It's good to be alone sometimes
and listen to music, read a good book,
or watch an old movie;
time to laugh, cry or be sad,
without having to explain,
glad to be alone,
guiltlessly alone.

It's good to be alone sometimes,
but other times it hurts.
The reminiscing is painful,
it brings regrets of times gone by,
answers provided, decisions made.

Even so, the feeling remains,
it's good to be alone...
sometimes.

I Wonder

From time to time
I wonder how it feels
when you look at
the young man or woman
standing before you,
so self-sufficient,
so well balanced,
living a life filled with
satisfactions & successes.
You probably think back
to what now seems
so long ago and
remember the sleepless nights,
the incessant crying,
the fevers, the cuts & bruises,
the doctor's crowded office.
Too soon those times were replaced
by a rebellious stranger;
cries of unfairness, tyranny or
dictatorship flourished
from one you did not recognize.
Then, not soon enough,
those moments also passed
and like the caterpillar,
this young person metamorphosed
into someone you actually like &
can talk to, even get along with.
Oh the grandeur of life's passages;
education, disappointments,
losses & successes
have obliged this person
to become more understanding,
patient & responsible.
And so, dear parent,
when looking at the young person
who is a part of you,
I imagine you feel proud, accomplished.

All those years of ups & downs
were worth it in the end.
Yes, these thoughts go through my mind...
sometimes...and...
I wonder how it feels.

Memories

One day, as I helped mother
clean her overflowing closet,
she reached into a dark corner
and pulled out a time worn
photo album brimming with memories.
We stopped our mission and
looked at reminders of
carefree summers, snowy winters,
holiday celebrations,
family and friends, forever young.

She turned pages without haste,
one, two, three, four...
She recalled names & told stories;
so many moments,
so many memories.
I asked about a handsome
young man in military uniform
standing next to her
beneath a *flamboyán* tree.
His arm is on her shoulder,
both are smiling & seem content.
She contemplated the photo
and remained quiet.
I sensed reticence.
Then she looked at me,
smiled with nostalgia & said,
Just a friend.

I wondered.
Who is he?
What really happened?
Decades have passed.
Mother claimed the truth.
I acquiesced.
No use arguing with memories.

Flamboyán – Poinciana tree

Childhood Remembrances

Sometimes I need to reconnect
with my childhood in Brooklyn.
The images that surface
make me feel all warm & peaceful inside.

I close my eyes and there we are,
my sister, my brother, & me,
in our secret hallway closet playing house.
The tea sets, mini pots & pans, dolls &
blankets are all around us.
The minutes & hours tick on,
but we don't care.
I don't want to open my eyes,
life was so simple back then.

I close my eyes again and there we are,
my sister, my brother, & me,
in the sun filled backyard,
under the garden hose
that Mom tied to the clothesline.
We squeal & jump up & down
as the cool water sprays
our hot & sweaty little bodies.
I wish I didn't have to open my eyes,
life was so sweet back then.

Sometimes I don't need to close my eyes.
When I sit in front of my Christmas tree,
alone in a shadowy, hushed house,
I am mesmerized by the sparkling lights and
soothing aroma of pine that permeates the air.
I remember the Christmases of long ago,
I even taste the anticipation,
the excitement of Christmas morning.
I hear the squeals of delight for
the dollhouse, the Lionel train set,
the flirty eyes doll;

everything we wished for was there!
Life was so blissful back then.

It seems I cannot let go of those moments,
or perhaps I don't want to let go.
All I know is that there are times,
in the midst of my life so hurried,
that I need to go back for an instant
to recapture and relive
the simple, sweet & blissful times,
for the child that reveled in them is alive &
yearns to be reminded that life is still good.

Safe Haven

I wake up startled!
There's a loud, cracking noise & rumble,
but my eyes only see darkness.
Suddenly, a flashing light,
an exploding, splintering noise
fills my room.
I peek out from under the blanket
and see eerie shadows dancing on the walls.
My heart is bursting, I hear rain pounding,
pounding, pounding, louder and louder.
I call out into the darkness that follows,
"Mom. Mom."
No answer.
I know their bedroom door is open,
like it is every night.
"Mom. Mom," I call out again
in a whimpering, loud whisper.
No response.
Light brightens my room once again,
the rumbling shakes the walls,
thunder follows close behind,
it sounds louder than before,
my voice too gets louder,
"Mom! Mom!"
Knowing full well what I want,
finally she responds, "What is it?"
"Can I go to your bed?"
Without argument or hesitation,
she agrees.
I jump out of bed, grab my blanket and run
into my parents' room.
Nimble & sprite, I climb up on the bed
and snuggle down deep between Mom & Dad.
Oh, what warmth & peace inundates me!
Flash! Rumble! Crack!
Outside, the storm continues,
rain pounds against the window panes

as if wanting to break them,
but I don't care.
I close my eyes and burrow deeper
into my niche;
nothing can happen to me here,
I'm in my safe haven.

Weaving Past and Present

There are many memories of persons, places and emotions
from my past that I love and hold captive in my heart;
memories that I visit and revisit whenever the need arises.
I thought that returning to those places and persons
would be like stepping into a room
where nothing has changed over time, but
I was wrong, life is not like that.

Where there once were many trees and multicolor foliage,
now there are houses, shopping centers, and super highways.
Where there once was a sandy beach I could stroll on,
now there are stones and rough terrains that are uninviting.
Where once conversations were about *joie de vivre*,
now center on reluctant aging, aches & pains.

Upon reflection, I realize that
as I go from one moment to the other,
from one experience to the other, I too change.
Whether I perceive it or not, I am different,
and in that same manner,
the people and places I love have also changed.

What should I do with my memories?
Should I adjust them? Should I keep them intact?
Should I abandon them and try to forget?
I choose to keep them,
for only in my mind, only in my memories
can all past moments and experiences remain the same,
like the photographs I treasure and feel compelled to
contemplate from time to time
because they comfort me.

I know that whenever I feel the need,
I will go back to those special moments
and enjoy them for a short while,
understanding that those threads
are part of my fabric, even though

some may have unraveled a bit.
I also know that today I am here,
I must live my present moment and
weave new memories between &
around the threads of the past.

CPSIA information can be obtained
at www.ICGtesting.com
Printed in the USA
FSHW021038091019
62759FS